Still In Love With Her: A Guide To Sustain in a Long-Term Relationship

Rajesh Giri

Published by Rajesh Giri, 2023.

While every precaution has been taken in the preparation of this book, the publisher assumes no responsibility for errors or omissions, or for damages resulting from the use of the information contained herein.

STILL IN LOVE WITH HER: A GUIDE TO SUSTAIN IN A LONG-TERM RELATIONSHIP

First edition. February 25, 2023.

ISBN: 979-8215406984

Written by Rajesh Giri.

Table of Contents

Dedicated To

I am honored to dedicate this book to my beloved parents, the late Shri Kanti Giri and late Shrimati Champa Devi. They were not only my parents but also my greatest mentors and role models, who instilled in me a love of learning and a passion for seeking the truth.

Their unwavering support and encouragement throughout my life have been invaluable to me, and I will be forever grateful for their love and guidance. Although they are no longer with us, their legacy lives on through this book and my continued pursuit of knowledge and understanding.

I hope that this book serves as a fitting tribute to their memory and the profound impact they had on my life.

Legal Disclaimer

Preface

Welcome to "The Science of Long-Term Love", a comprehensive guide to understanding and nurturing love in long-term relationships. Whether you are just starting out or have been together for years, this book will provide you with valuable insights, practical tips, and strategies for navigating the ups and downs of love.

Written by Rajesh Kumar Giri, in the field, this book offers a unique blend of practical research, personal experiences, and real-world examples to help you cultivate a healthy, fulfilling, and lasting relationship.

With chapters covering everything from communication and conflict resolution to intimacy and personal growth, you'll gain a deep understanding of what it takes to make love last.

I believe that love is a journey that requires patience, understanding, and effort, and I am thrilled to be your guide along the way. Whether you are seeking to improve your current relationship or are looking for guidance in starting a new one, "The Science of Long-Term Love" will provide you with the tools you need to create a loving and fulfilling partnership.

So sit back, grab a cup of coffee, and let's dive into the fascinating world of long-term love together.

With Love

Rajesh Kumar Giri

Open Talk with Rajesh Kumar Giri

Long-term relationships are complex, and being still in love with someone after years or even decades can be both fulfilling and challenging. In "Still in Love: Navigating the Complexities of Long-Term Love," we explore what it means to sustain love over time, and offer insights and strategies for couples who want to deepen their connection and build a lasting relationship.

I am not going to pitch you only about the love with your so called baby. It is all about the real and fascinating love with anyone who really cares about your emotion, your privacy, your decisions and your passion.

LET US START WITH A poem I love

I thought I moved on, left her in the past,
But my heart still beats for her, it beats so fast,
Though I tried to forget, she's still on my mind,
I can't help but wonder, if she feels the same kind.
I see her in my dreams, in every thought,
I feel her in my heart, it can't be fought,

For she's the one who got away, but not really,
For in my heart she stays, it's the truth, verily.
I've loved and lost, but this love remains,
A constant ache, a feeling that sustains,
I've tried to move on, but my heart won't budge,
For she's the only one, my heart won't judge.
Still in love with her, it's a fact I can't deny,
I'll always love her, till the day I die,
For she's the one who stole my heart, my soul,
And I'll love her forever, that's my ultimate goal.

In this book, I have tried to explain my practical experiences and in psychology, neuroscience, and relationship studies, as well as the experiences of real couples, to explore the dynamics of long-term love.

I delve into topics such as the evolution of love in a relationship, recognizing the signs of a long-term love, and the power of communication in sustaining love.

I also offer practical strategies for reigniting passion, managing conflict, and balancing individuality and togetherness.

Whether you're in a long-term relationship, or just starting out on your journey together, "Still in Love" offers a wealth of insights and inspiration for anyone seeking to build a lasting, fulfilling relationship.

With Love

Rajesh Kumar Giri

(The Practical Success Coach)

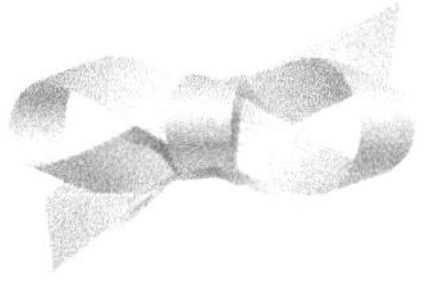

Chapter 1: The Science of Long-Term Love

LOVE IS ONE OF THE most complex and fascinating human emotions. It can bring great joy and fulfillment to our lives, but it can also be a source of pain and disappointment. For many of us, finding and maintaining a long-term romantic relationship is one of our most significant life goals.

So before discussing anything just recite this poem and feel the fact.

Love is not a mystery, nor just a feeling,
It's a chemical reaction, the brain revealing,
Oxytocin, dopamine, and serotonin play a part,
The science of love, unlocking the heart.

But what is the secret to making love last?

While it's a question that has puzzled humans for centuries, modern science has shed new light on the dynamics of long-term love. Researchers have identified several key factors that contribute to sustaining a loving relationship over time.

Research suggests that there are several factors that contribute to long-term love, including the chemistry that underlies our emotional and physical connections. In this article, we will explore the science of long-term love and provide insights into how you can build and maintain a strong, healthy relationship.

Understanding the Chemistry of Love

The chemical reactions that occur in our brains when we fall in love have been the subject of much scientific research. One of the most famous studies in this field was conducted by Helen Fisher, a biological anthropologist at Rutgers University. She identified three key chemicals that are involved in the process of falling in love: dopamine, norepinephrine, and serotonin.

Dopamine is a neurotransmitter that is associated with pleasure and reward. When we are in the early stages of a romantic relationship, our brains release high levels of dopamine, which makes us feel euphoric and motivated to pursue our partner.

Norepinephrine is a hormone that is linked to the "fight or flight" response. It increases our heart rate, elevates our blood pressure, and makes us feel jittery and excited. Finally, serotonin is a neurotransmitter that helps regulate our moods and emotions. Low levels of serotonin have been associated with obsessive thinking and compulsive behavior, which can be a characteristic of early-stage romantic love.

While these chemicals play a significant role in the initial stages of falling in love, they are not enough to sustain a long-term relationship. Over time, the brain chemistry associated with romantic love gives way to a more stable set of chemicals that help to deepen our emotional and physical connections with our partner.

Building a Strong Relationship

So, if chemistry alone is not enough to keep love alive, what are the other factors that contribute to a long and healthy relationship?

Research suggests that there are several key elements that help to build and maintain a strong partnership.

One of the most important factors is communication

Effective communication is essential for any relationship to thrive. It is important to be open and honest with your partner about your needs, wants, and feelings.

It is also essential to listen actively to your partner and to be willing to compromise when necessary.

Another critical factor is shared values and goals. It is important to have a common understanding of what you both want out of life and to work together to achieve those goals. This can help to create a sense of shared purpose and can help to strengthen your emotional connection.

Trust a Fundamental Component of Healthy Relationship

Trust is built over time through consistent and reliable behavior. It is important to be honest with your partner and to keep your promises. When trust is broken, it can be difficult to repair, so it is essential to prioritize trust in your relationship.

It is important to nurture the physical and emotional connection between you and your partner. This can involve engaging in activities that you both enjoy, taking time to be intimate with one another, and expressing appreciation and gratitude for your partner.

Role of attachment

Attachment theory suggests that the bond between two people in a relationship is rooted in our earliest experiences with attachment figures, usually our parents. The quality of these early attachments can shape our patterns of attachment in adult relationships, and influence how we respond to our partner's needs and emotions.

Concept of Positive Illusions

Positive illusions refer to the way we view our partner through rose-colored glasses, seeing them as better and more perfect than they actually are. While some might argue that this is a form of self-deception, research suggests that positive illusions can actually enhance relationship satisfaction and stability.

Finally, scientists have identified the importance of shared experiences and memories in sustaining long-term love. Couples who have a rich history of shared experiences and positive memories are more likely to stay together over time, and to report higher levels of relationship satisfaction.

Conclusion

The science of long-term love is complex, but it offers valuable insights into how we can build and maintain strong, healthy relationships.

By understanding the chemical reactions that underlie our emotional and physical connections, and by prioritizing effective communication, shared values, trust, and physical and emotional intimacy, we can create relationships that last a lifetime.

While there's no magic formula for sustaining love over time, understanding the science of long-term love can help couples build a stronger, more resilient relationship.

By cultivating a secure attachment, fostering positive illusions, and creating shared experiences, couples can deepen their connection and build a love that lasts.

Chapter 2: The Evolution of Love in a Relationship

LOVE IS NOT A STATIC emotion, but rather a dynamic force that changes and evolves over time. In the early stages of a relationship, love is often characterized by passion, infatuation, and intense feelings of attraction. However, as the relationship progresses, love may take on different forms, such as deep companionship, loyalty, and commitment.

One reason for this evolution is that the brain chemistry of love changes over time. The early stages of a relationship are marked by high levels of dopamine and other neurotransmitters that create feelings of euphoria and excitement. However, as the relationship progresses, these chemicals decrease, and other neurotransmitters, such as oxytocin, become more prominent. Oxytocin is often referred to as the "cuddle hormone," as it is associated with feelings of closeness, intimacy, and bonding.

Love is an intricate and multifaceted concept, and its evolution in a long-term relationship can be a fascinating topic to explore. Understanding the science behind the evolution of love can help couples cultivate and maintain a healthy and lasting relationship.

Love in the beginning, a spark ignites,
Two hearts beating, with passion so bright,
But as time goes on, the spark dims,
And love evolves, into something within.
The excitement of new love fades away,
But something deeper, comes out to play,
A love that's built, on trust and respect,
A bond that's strong, and hard to neglect.
The little things, become so important,
A kind gesture, a smile, an endearment,
A simple touch, can ignite the flame,
And love, once again, will take aim.
Love in a relationship, is not just one thing,
It's an evolution that keeps on giving
It's a journey, that two hearts embark,
And a love that grows, as they leave their mark.
Through ups and downs, and highs and lows,
Love evolves, and only grows;
It's a beautiful thing, that two hearts share,
An evolution of love, that's beyond compare.

Stages of Love

Love is not a static emotion; it evolves over time. Psychologist Robert Sternberg developed a model of love consisting of three main components: intimacy, passion, and commitment. According to his theory, the intensity of these components can fluctuate, leading to different stages of love.

The first stage: infatuation stage

The first stage is the infatuation stage, also known as the honeymoon stage. In this stage, the intimacy and passion components are high, while commitment is low. Couples in this stage often feel a strong attraction towards each other, and everything seems perfect.

The second stage: attachment stage

In this stage, the intimacy and commitment components are high, while passion may decline. Couples in this stage feel a deep sense of attachment and commitment to each other. They may not feel the intense passion that they felt in the infatuation stage, but they have a strong emotional bond that is based on shared experiences and a deep understanding of each other.

The third stage: mature love stage

The third stage is the mature love stage. In this stage, all three components of love (intimacy, passion, and commitment) are balanced and present in a healthy relationship. Couples in this stage have a deep sense of connection, trust, and commitment to each other. Their love has evolved into a deeper and more mature form, based on a shared life together.

Ways to Strengthen the Bond between Partners

While every relationship is unique, there are some general strategies that can help couples strengthen their bond and maintain a healthy and lasting relationship.

One key strategy is to cultivate emotional intimacy. Emotional intimacy involves sharing feelings, thoughts, and experiences with each other. It helps couples feel connected and understood, and it can strengthen the emotional bond between partners.

Another strategy is to engage in shared experiences. Shared experiences can include anything from traveling together to taking a cooking class. They help couples build memories and create a sense of shared identity, which can strengthen their bond and enhance their emotional connection.

Conclusion

Love is a complex emotion that evolves over time. Understanding the science behind the evolution of love can help couples cultivate and maintain a healthy and lasting relationship.

By focusing on emotional intimacy, effective communication, and shared experiences, couples can strengthen their bond and deepen their love for each other.

Despite the changes that occur over time, however, love can continue to deepen and flourish throughout a long-term relationship.

Couples who are willing to adapt and grow together, and who are committed to maintaining a strong emotional connection, are more likely to experience the enduring joy and fulfillment that come with a lasting love.

Chapter 3: Recognizing the Signs of a Long-Term Love

HOW DO YOU KNOW IF you're in a long-term love?

While the experience of love can be highly subjective, there are several key indicators that suggest a relationship has the potential to last.

A love that lasts, is more than just a feeling,
It's built on trust, and mutual revealing,
It's not just about, the passion and the heat,
But a bond that's strong, and hard to defeat.
It's in the little things, like holding hands,
And being there, to help make plans,
It's a love that grows, with each passing day,
And recognizing the signs can show you the way.

One important sign is a shared sense of purpose or vision for the future. Couples who are aligned in their values, goals, and dreams are more likely to stay together and weather the challenges that come their way.

Similarly, couples who have a strong emotional connection and a deep level of intimacy are more likely to experience a lasting love.

Couples who are able to listen to each other, express their needs and emotions clearly, and work together to find mutually satisfying solutions are more likely to stay together and avoid the patterns of disconnection and resentment that can erode a relationship over time.

While no relationship is perfect, recognizing these signs can help couples build a stronger foundation for a lasting love.

As I've discussed earlier, long-term love is something that develops over time, and it requires a strong foundation of mutual respect, trust, and communication.

But how do you know if you're in a long-term love relationship? Here are some signs to look out for:

1. **You Can Be Yourself:** In a long-term love relationship, you feel comfortable being your true self around your partner. You don't feel the need to put on a facade or hide your true feelings. Your partner accepts you for who you are flaws and all.

2. **You Communicate Openly:** Communication is key in any relationship, and it's especially important in a long-term love relationship. You and your partner are able to talk about anything and everything, even the tough stuff. You feel heard and understood, and you make an effort to listen to your partner as well.

3. **You Support Each Other:** In a long-term love relationship, you and your partner are each other's biggest cheerleaders. You support each other through the ups and downs, and you're there for each other no matter what.

4. **You Have Shared Values:** While it's okay to have some

differences in a relationship, having shared values is important for a long-term love to thrive. You and your partner are on the same page when it comes to things like family, finances, and future goals.

5. **You Have Fun Together:** Even after years together, you still find ways to have fun with each other. Whether it's trying a new hobby or revisiting an old one, you enjoy spending time with your partner and making memories together.

If you're experiencing these signs, then congratulations! You're likely in a long-term love relationship. But remember, relationships take work, and it's important to continue to nurture your connection with your partner over time.

Tips for Maintaining a Long-Term Love Relationship

Let's explore some tips for maintaining that connection over time.

1. **Keep Communicating:** As I mentioned earlier, communication is key in any relationship. Make an effort to check in with your partner regularly, even if it's just a quick "How was your day?" text. Take the time to really listen to your partner and validate their feelings.

2. **Show Appreciation:** It's easy to take your partner for granted after years together, but it's important to continue showing them appreciation. Thank them for the things they do for you, no matter how small, and let them know how much you value them.

3. **Keep the Romance Alive:** Just because you've been together for a long time doesn't mean you should let the romance fade away. Plan date nights, surprise each other with thoughtful gestures, and make an effort to keep things exciting in the bedroom.

4. **Respect Each Other's Space:** While it's important to spend quality time together, it's also important to respect each other's

individual space. Encourage each other to pursue hobbies and interests, and make sure you have some alone time as well.

5. **Work as a Team:** In a long-term love relationship, you and your partner are a team. Make decisions together, support each other's goals, and work through challenges as a united front.

6. **Be Forgiving:** No one is perfect, and mistakes will happen. It's important to be able to forgive each other and move forward. Holding onto grudges will only create resentment and distance between you and your partner.

Remember, a long-term love relationship takes effort and dedication, but the rewards are worth it. By following these tips, you can help ensure that your love continues to thrive for years to come.

Chapter 4: The Power of Communication in Sustaining Love

Effective communication is a cornerstone of any successful relationship, but it's especially important in long-term love. As a relationship evolves over time, communication can become more complex, with a wider range of emotions, needs, and expectations to navigate.

Poem is enough to explain everything you need to feel.

Words are powerful; in love they play a crucial role,
Communication, the bridge that connects two souls,
A heart that listens, and a voice that speaks,
An open dialogue, that brings the love to its peak.
Through good times and bad, communication is key,
It helps us understand, and helps us to see,
The needs and desires, of our loved one's heart,

And how we can support, right from the start.
When we communicate, we build trust and respect,
We open up our hearts, and let love intersect,
For love to thrive, it needs a voice to be heard,
And the power of communication is love's magic word.

Communication is often touted as the key to a successful relationship, and for good reason. In a long-term love relationship, the ability to communicate openly and honestly with your partner is essential for building trust, resolving conflicts, and staying connected over time.

One of the biggest benefits of good communication is that it helps prevent misunderstandings. When you and your partner are able to express your thoughts and feelings clearly and respectfully, you're less likely to misinterpret each other's actions or intentions. This can help prevent unnecessary arguments and misunderstandings that can cause tension and distance in a relationship.

Another benefit of communication is that it helps build intimacy. By sharing your innermost thoughts, fears, and desires with your partner, you create a deeper emotional bond that can help sustain your love over time. When you feel comfortable opening up to your partner, it can help foster a sense of emotional safety and security that's essential for maintaining a healthy, long-term relationship.

Good communication can also help you navigate challenges more effectively. When you and your partner are able to communicate openly and respectfully, you're better equipped to work together to find solutions to problems. Whether you're dealing with a minor disagreement or a major life event, being able to communicate effectively can help you get through it together.

Of course, communication isn't always easy. It can be difficult to express your thoughts and feelings, especially when you're feeling vulnerable or upset. But the effort is worth it. By prioritizing good communication in your relationship, you can help ensure that your love continues to thrive and grow over time.

In conclusion, communication is a powerful tool for sustaining love in a long-term relationship. By making an effort to communicate openly and honestly with your partner, you can build trust, prevent misunderstandings, foster intimacy, and navigate challenges more effectively.

Tips for communication to sustain in love

- **Practice active listening:** When your partner is speaking, make an effort to really listen and understand what they're saying. This means giving them your full attention, making eye contact, and avoiding interrupting or judging.

- **Use "I" statements:** When expressing your thoughts or feelings, use "I" statements instead of "you" statements. For example, say "I feel hurt when..." instead of "You always make me feel hurt when..."

- **Avoid criticism and defensiveness:** Criticizing your partner or becoming defensive when they express their feelings can quickly escalate into an argument. Instead, try to approach the conversation with empathy and a desire to understand their perspective.

- **Take breaks when needed:** If the conversation becomes too heated or emotional, it's okay to take a break and come back to it later. This can help both partners calm down and approach the conversation with a clearer mind.

- **Don't avoid difficult conversations:** While it may be tempting to avoid difficult topics or conversations, doing so can cause resentment and distance in the relationship. Instead, make an effort to address the issue in a calm and respectful way.

- **Practice forgiveness:** No one is perfect, and mistakes and misunderstandings are bound to happen. When they do, practice forgiveness and make an effort to move forward instead of holding onto grudges.

- **Show appreciation:** Communication isn't just about addressing problems or conflicts. It's also important to express appreciation and gratitude for your partner and the positive aspects of your relationship. Letting your partner know you value and appreciate them can help strengthen your bond over time.

By incorporating these tips into your communication with your partner, you can help ensure that your love continues to thrive and grow over time.

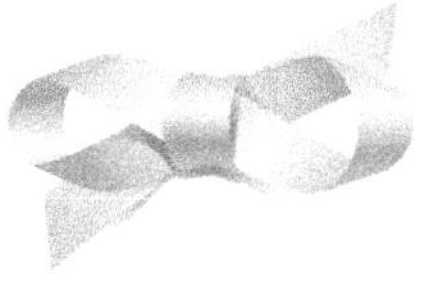

Chapter 5: Navigating Change and Transition

LIFE IS FULL OF CHANGE and transition, and these can be particularly challenging in a long-term relationship. Whether it's a major life event such as a job loss, a move to a new city, or the birth of a child, or a gradual shift in priorities or interests, couples need to be able to adapt and grow together in order to sustain their love over time.

Feel the love before you learn.

Love is not static, it's ever-changing,
Through seasons of life, it keeps rearranging,
We grow and evolve, as time moves on,
And love must adapt, for it to stay strong.
Transitions can be hard; they can bring on stress,
But in long-term love, we learn to address,

The changes that come, with an open heart,
And support each other, from the very start.
It's not always easy, to navigate change,
But in love, we find a way to arrange,
Our lives together, in a new normal,
And our love grows deeper, in the midst of the tumult.
For in long-term love, we learn to be flexible,
To adapt to change, and make it workable,
And in doing so, we find a new way,
To love each other, every single day.

One key to navigating change and transition in long-term love is to maintain open communication and a willingness to be flexible. This means being willing to listen to each other's needs and perspectives, and to make adjustments and compromises as necessary to accommodate changing circumstances.

Another important factor is to maintain a sense of emotional connection and intimacy, even during times of stress or upheaval. This can involve carving out dedicated time for each other, such as date nights or shared hobbies, as well as being intentional about expressing affection and appreciation on a regular basis.

Finally, it's important to recognize that change and transition can also present opportunities for growth and renewal in a long-term relationship. By facing challenges together and adapting to new circumstances, couples can deepen their emotional bond and create a stronger foundation for a lasting love.

As with any aspect of life, change and transition are inevitable in long-term love relationships. Whether it's a new job, a move to a new city, the birth of a child, or any other major life event, navigating these changes together can be a challenge.

Tips for handling change and transition in a long-term love relationship:

- **Communicate openly:** As always, communication is key. Make an effort to discuss any upcoming changes or transitions, how you feel about them, and what you both can do to support each other during the transition.
- **Be patient and understanding:** Change can be stressful and emotional, so it's important to be patient and understanding with each other. Recognize that you both may have different ways of coping with the change, and be willing to compromise and support each other.
- **Find ways to stay connected:** When going through a major change or transition, it's easy to feel disconnected from each other. Make an effort to find ways to stay connected, whether it's setting aside time to talk or finding new shared activities to enjoy together.
- **Practice self-care:** Change and transition can be overwhelming, so it's important to take care of you during this time. Make sure you're getting enough sleep, exercise, and eating well. Also, take time to do things you enjoy and that help you relax.
- **Seek outside help if needed:** If you're having trouble navigating the change or transition on your own, don't be afraid to seek outside help. This could be a couples therapist, a life coach, or even a trusted friend or family member.
- **Remember your love and commitment:** During times of change and transition, it's easy to lose sight of your love and commitment to each other. Make an effort to remember why you fell in love and what you're committed to in your relationship.

By approaching change and transition with open communication, patience, and understanding, you can navigate these challenges together and come out stronger on the other side.

Chapter 6: The Role of Forgiveness

FORGIVENESS IS AN ESSENTIAL aspect of any long-term relationship. It involves letting go of past hurt and resentment and moving forward with a renewed sense of love and understanding.

Without forgiveness, a relationship can quickly deteriorate and lead to a breakdown in communication and trust. In this section, we will explore the role of forgiveness in long-term love.

In love, forgiveness is key,

To keep the flame burning steadily,

For hearts are bound to err and stray,

But forgiveness paves a better way.

It mends the cracks in fragile hearts,

And fosters love that never departs,

Forgiveness nurtures a love that's true,

And makes it last, like morning dew.
So let forgiveness be your guide,
In love, let grace and mercy abide,
For in its embrace, love will endure,
And forevermore, it shall be pure.

Forgiveness is a choice that is made by both partners in a relationship.

It requires the willingness to let go of the past and move forward without holding grudges or resentments. Forgiveness is not always easy, and it may take time and effort to work through past hurt and pain. However, the benefits of forgiveness are immeasurable and can help to strengthen the bond between partners.

One of the primary benefits of forgiveness is that it allows both partners to let go of negative emotions and move forward with a renewed sense of love and commitment.

Forgiveness helps to create a safe and nurturing environment where both partners can be vulnerable and open with each other. This level of emotional intimacy is critical for a long-term relationship and can help to deepen the bond between partners.

Another benefit of forgiveness is that it helps to build trust between partners. When one partner forgives the other, it shows that they are committed to the relationship and are willing to work through any challenges that may arise. This level of commitment and trust is essential for a long-term relationship and can help to create a sense of security and stability for both partners.

To cultivate forgiveness in your relationship, it's important to communicate openly and honestly with your partner. Be willing to listen to their perspective and try to understand where they are coming from. Take responsibility for your actions and apologize when necessary. It's also important to set healthy boundaries and make sure that both partners feel respected and heard.

Tips for cultivating forgiveness in your relationship:

- Communicate openly and honestly with your partner
- Be willing to listen to their perspective
- Take responsibility for your actions
- Apologize when necessary
- Set healthy boundaries
- Practice empathy and understanding
- Focus on the present moment and let go of the past

In conclusion, forgiveness is an essential aspect of any long-term relationship. It helps to build trust, deepen emotional intimacy, and create a sense of security and stability.

By cultivating forgiveness in your relationship, you can help to strengthen your bond with your partner and create a fulfilling and lasting love.

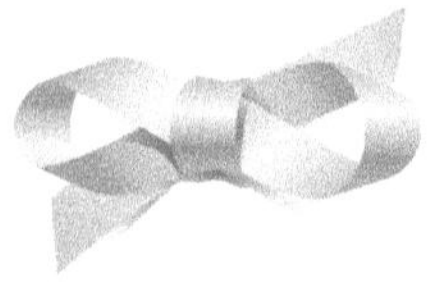

Chapter 7: The Importance of Intimacy

INTIMACY IS A VITAL component of any long-term relationship, but its meaning and expression can evolve over time. In the early stages of a relationship, intimacy is often characterized by physical passion and excitement. However, as a relationship matures, intimacy can take on deeper and more meaningful forms, such as emotional connection, vulnerability, and mutual support.

Intimacy plays a crucial role in long-term love. As the years go by, it can be easy to fall into a routine and forget about the importance of connecting with your partner on a deeper level. However, neglecting intimacy can lead to feelings of loneliness and disconnection in the relationship.

In the depths of love, where hearts entwine,
Intimacy reigns supreme, divine,

For in each other's arms, we find,
A love that's pure, and truly kind.
Intimacy, the soul of love,
A connection that's felt, not just thought of,
A bond that's strong, and ever-growing,
Through life's ups and downs, it keeps us flowing.
For in the moments when we're close,
Our love is strengthened, and it glows,
Our hearts beat as one, our souls entwine,
Intimacy, the ultimate sign.
So let us cherish, each moment of closeness,
For it's in these moments, we find wholeness,
Intimacy, the cornerstone of love
The thread that binds us, and soars above.

Reasons why intimacy is essential in long-term love:

1. **Emotional Connection:** Intimacy helps to create a deep emotional connection with your partner. It allows you to share your innermost thoughts, feelings, and desires with each other. This emotional connection is what sets apart romantic relationships from friendships and is vital for a long-lasting bond.

2. **Physical Connection:** Physical intimacy is an essential aspect of any romantic relationship. It helps to strengthen the emotional bond and creates a sense of security and comfort in the relationship. Physical touch, such as cuddling, holding hands, and kissing, releases the hormone oxytocin, which creates feelings of closeness and connection.

3. **Improved Communication:** When you are intimate with your partner, you learn to communicate on a deeper level. It helps you to understand your partner's needs and desires and can lead to better communication in other aspects of your relationship.

4. **Increased Trust:** Intimacy creates trust and helps to build a strong foundation in your relationship. When you share your vulnerabilities and desires with your partner, it creates a safe space for both of you to be open and honest.

5. **Stress Relief:** Being intimate with your partner can help to relieve stress and promote relaxation. It releases endorphins, which are natural painkillers, and helps to reduce anxiety and tension.

In conclusion, intimacy is a crucial component of a long-term love relationship. It creates an emotional and physical connection, improves communication, increases trust, and promotes stress relief.

By prioritizing intimacy in your relationship, you can strengthen your bond and create a fulfilling and lasting love connection.

Tips that can help promote intimacy in your long-term relationship

1. **Prioritize quality time together:** Spend uninterrupted time with your partner, free from distractions such as phones, work, or other obligations. Make time for activities that both of you enjoy and that allow you to connect with each other.

2. **Engage in physical touch:** Physical touch can be an important way to promote intimacy in a long-term relationship. Whether it's holding hands, hugging, or cuddling, these small acts of physical touch can help strengthen your bond.

3. **Practice open and honest communication:** Communication is key to any healthy relationship, including intimacy. Talk openly with your partner about your feelings, desires, and needs. Be honest and open about your thoughts and feelings towards each other.

4. **Be attentive to each other's needs:** Being attentive to each other's needs can show your partner that you care and are invested in the relationship. Make an effort to understand and

meet each other's emotional and physical needs.

5. **Create new experiences together:** Trying new experiences together can be an exciting way to promote intimacy and create new memories. Whether it's traveling to a new place or trying a new hobby, these shared experiences can help deepen your connection with each other.

6. **Be supportive and understanding:** In a long-term relationship, it's important to be supportive and understanding of each other's challenges and goals. Show empathy towards your partner's struggles and celebrate each other's successes.

By following these tips, you can help promote intimacy and strengthen your long-term love relationship. Remember, intimacy requires effort and commitment, but the rewards are worth it.

Chapter 8: Cultivating Gratitude and Appreciation

GRATITUDE AND APPRECIATION are powerful tools for maintaining a positive and fulfilling long-term relationship. By actively cultivating a sense of gratitude and appreciation for your partner, you can deepen your emotional connection and create a more fulfilling and satisfying love.

In the garden of love, where emotions bloom,
Gratitude and appreciation, our hearts consume,
For in the light of thankfulness, we see,
The beauty of love, and its majesty.
Through the ups and downs of life's journey,
Gratitude and appreciation, our love's attorney,
They help us see the goodness in each other,

And cherish the love we have, forever.
For when we cultivate an attitude of thankfulness,
Love blossoms, and becomes more precious,
We see the little things that make us smile,
And appreciate them, for a little while.
So let us water the garden of our love,
With gratitude and appreciation, like a dove,
For they bring forth a love that's pure and true,
A love that lasts forever, me and you.

One key to cultivating gratitude and appreciation is to be intentional about recognizing and acknowledging your partner's positive qualities and actions. This can involve expressing gratitude for everyday gestures, such as cooking dinner or doing the dishes, as well as more significant contributions to the relationship, such as emotional support during a difficult time.

Another important aspect of gratitude and appreciation is to be willing to focus on the positive aspects of your partner and relationship, even during difficult times. This means consciously choosing to see the good in your partner and the relationship, rather than dwelling on negative experiences or emotions.

Ultimately, cultivating gratitude and appreciation in long-term love can help couples create a more positive and fulfilling emotional connection, and can deepen their sense of commitment and mutual support.

Expressing gratitude and appreciation for your partner is an essential aspect of long-term love. These acts of kindness and appreciation create a positive atmosphere in the relationship and help to deepen the bond between the partners.

Cultivating gratitude and appreciation can also contribute to a more optimistic and loving outlook, which can help to overcome the inevitable difficulties that arise in any relationship.

Tips on how to cultivate gratitude and appreciation

1. **Start with yourself:** Before you can express gratitude and appreciation for your partner, it's important to appreciate yourself. Recognize your own qualities and strengths and express gratitude for your own abilities and accomplishments.
2. **Look for the good:** Focus on the positive aspects of your partner and your relationship. Make a conscious effort to notice the good things your partner does and express appreciation for them.
3. **Be specific:** When expressing gratitude and appreciation, be specific about what you are thankful for. Instead of saying "thank you for everything," say "thank you for doing the dishes last night, it really helped me out."
4. **Show your appreciation:** Don't just express your appreciation in words, show it through your actions. Do something special for your partner to show them that you appreciate them.
5. **Practice daily gratitude:** Take a few minutes each day to reflect on what you are grateful for in your relationship. This can be done alone or with your partner.

By cultivating gratitude and appreciation in your relationship, you can create a positive and loving environment that will help your long-term love to flourish.

It's important to remember that expressing gratitude and appreciation is not just a one-time thing, but a daily practice that can help to strengthen your bond with your partner.

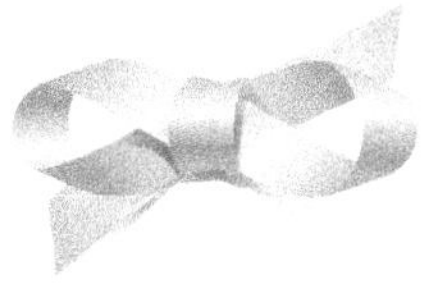

Chapter 9: The Importance of Personal Growth and Development

Personal growth and development are essential components of any healthy relationship, but they are especially important in long-term love. As individuals evolve and change over time, it's important for couples to be able to adapt and grow together in order to maintain a strong emotional connection.

In the journey of love, where hearts unite,
Personal growth and development, bring new light,
For when we strive to become our best selves,
Love thrives, and its beauty delves.
Through the twists and turns of life's path,
Personal growth and development, our love's staff,
They help us evolve, and become more,
And see the potential, in what we adore.
For when we focus on personal growth,

Our love expands, and becomes more loath,
We learn to communicate, and understand,
And build a love, that's truly grand.
So let us strive, to grow and develop,
And let our love, be truly enveloped,
For personal growth, brings love to new heights,
A love that lasts forever, and ignites.

Long-term love relationships are built on the foundation of trust, respect, and growth. As individuals, we are constantly evolving, learning, and changing.

It is important to recognize that personal growth and development play a crucial role in the success of a long-term love relationship.

When we prioritize our personal growth, we become better partners and contribute to the growth of the relationship as a whole.

Tips for cultivating personal growth and development

1. **Set personal goals:** It is important to have individual goals in a relationship. This not only helps in personal growth but also helps in building a strong foundation for the relationship. Share your goals with your partner and encourage them to do the same.

2. **Pursue your passions:** Pursuing your passions and interests is a great way to achieve personal growth. Encourage your partner to do the same and support each other's interests.

3. **Communicate openly:** Communication is key in any relationship. Openly communicate your thoughts, feelings, and aspirations with your partner. This helps in understanding each other's needs and goals, and can lead to personal growth.

4. **Seek feedback:** Seek feedback from your partner on how you can improve and grow as an individual. This will not only help you in your personal growth but also strengthen your relationship.

5. **Embrace change:** Embracing change is an important aspect of

personal growth. Be open to change and new experiences. This will help you in expanding your horizons and growing as an individual.

Personal growth and development are ongoing processes, and it is important to make them a priority in a long-term love relationship. By prioritizing personal growth, individuals can become better partners and contribute to the success and growth of the relationship as a whole.

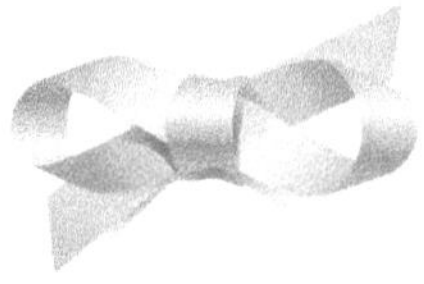

Chapter 10: Navigating Differences

DIFFERENCES AND CONFLICTS are inevitable in any relationship, but they can be particularly challenging in long-term love. Whether it differences in personality, values, or interests, couples need to be able to navigate these differences in a constructive and positive way in order to maintain a strong emotional connection over time.

It's not uncommon for couples to have differences and disagreements, whether it's in regards to values, beliefs, or preferences. However, it's how those differences are handled that can make or break a long-term love relationship.

Navigating differences can be challenging, but it's an important aspect of any relationship that needs to be addressed to sustain a healthy and long-lasting connection.

In the ocean of love, where waves collide,

Differences can arise, and often subside,
But when we navigate them with grace,
Love thrives, and finds its rightful place.
Through the ebbs and flows of life's tide,
Differences may come, and try to divide,
But when we approach them with an open heart,
Love blossoms, and never falls apart.
For when we embrace our unique ways,
Our love deepens, and forever stays,
We learn to appreciate, and understand,
And build a love, that's truly grand.
So let us navigate our differences with care,
And let our love, forever flourish and share,
For in the journey of love, we grow and thrive,
And find joy in the differences that keep our love alive.

Tips for navigating differences

1. **Practice active listening:** One of the most important skills in any relationship is active listening. This means not only hearing what your partner is saying, but truly listening and understanding their perspective. When you practice active listening, you can acknowledge your partner's feelings and validate their experiences, even if you don't necessarily agree with them.

2. **Respect differences:** It's important to respect your partner's opinions, even if they differ from your own. Remember that everyone has their own unique experiences and perspectives, and just because you disagree with someone doesn't mean that they're wrong. Respectful communication is key to navigating differences in a long-term love relationship.

3. **Find common ground:** While you may have differences, it's important to find common ground and shared values. This can help to bridge the gap between your differences and create a

sense of unity in your relationship. Try to focus on the things that you both enjoy and agree on, and use those as a foundation for your relationship.

4. **Don't make assumptions:** It's easy to assume that you know what your partner is thinking or feeling, but this can lead to misunderstandings and hurt feelings. Instead of making assumptions, ask your partner to clarify their thoughts and feelings. This can help to prevent misunderstandings and foster open communication.

5. **Compromise:** In any relationship, compromise is key. You may not always get your way, but it's important to find a solution that works for both partners. This means being willing to make concessions and finding a middle ground that you both can agree on.

Navigating differences in long-term love requires patience, respect, and communication. By practicing active listening, finding common ground, and being willing to compromise, you can build a strong and healthy relationship with your partner.

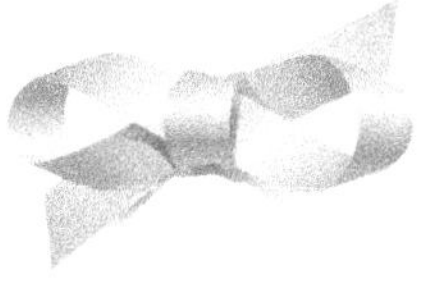

Chapter 11: Managing Conflict

Conflict is an inevitable part of any relationship, and long-term love is no exception. However, the way that couples manage conflict can have a significant impact on the health and longevity of the relationship.

Conflict is a natural part of any relationship, including long-term love. It is important to note that disagreements can arise from various issues such as misunderstandings, differences in opinions, or unmet needs.

However, how we handle these conflicts determines the overall success of the relationship.

> In the dance of love, where hearts entwine,
> Conflict can arise, and make us pine,
> But when we manage it with care,
> Love grows stronger, and we become a pair.
> Through the highs and lows of life's dance,

Conflict may come, and take a chance,
But when we approach it with love,
Our hearts unite, like hand in glove.
For when we handle conflict with grace,
Our love deepens, and we find our place,
We learn to communicate, and understand,
And build a love, that's truly grand.
So let us manage conflict with care,
And let our love, forever flourish and share,
For in the journey of love, we grow and thrive,
And find joy in the conflicts that keep our love alive.

In this section, we will discuss some tips for managing conflicts in long-term love.

1. Practice Active Listening

Active listening involves paying close attention to your partner when they are speaking, without interrupting or planning your response. It is important to understand your partner's perspective fully before responding. Active listening promotes empathy and understanding in a relationship, which is crucial in conflict resolution.

1. Express Yourself Clearly and Calmly

When discussing conflicts, it is important to express yourself in a clear and calm manner. Avoid using accusatory language, and instead focus on expressing your feelings and needs. This can help your partner understand where you are coming from and promote a healthy discussion.

1. Take a Break

Sometimes, conflicts can become overwhelming, and it may be necessary to take a break. This break can provide both partners with time to reflect on the situation and cool down. It is important to set a time to return to the discussion so that the issue is not left unresolved.

1. Compromise

Compromise involves finding a middle ground that satisfies both partners. It is important to recognize that not all conflicts have a clear winner or loser. Instead, both partners should work towards a solution that is mutually beneficial.

1. Seek Professional Help

If conflicts persist, it may be helpful to seek professional help. A therapist or counselor can provide objective support and guidance to help resolve conflicts and promote healthy communication.

Overall, managing conflicts in long-term love requires patience, active listening, and clear communication. By implementing these tips, conflicts can be resolved in a healthy and constructive manner, strengthening the bond between partners.

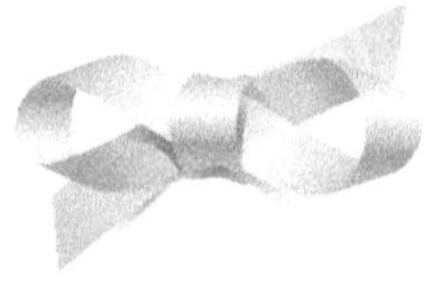

Chapter 12: Balancing Autonomy and Interdependence

Balancing autonomy and interdependence is an essential aspect of any healthy relationship, but it can be particularly challenging in long-term love. As couples navigate changing roles and responsibilities, it's important to find a balance between maintaining individual autonomy and fostering a deep emotional connection.

In the dance of love, where hearts are intertwined,
Autonomy and interdependence, can both be aligned,
For when we balance them with care,
Love grows stronger, and we become a pair.
Through the twists and turns of life's dance,
Autonomy and interdependence, can take a chance,
But when we approach them with love,

Our hearts unite, like hand in glove.
For when we balance our needs and desires,
Our love deepens, and our passion inspires,
We learn to trust and to depend,
And build a love that will never end.
So let us balance autonomy and interdependence,
And let our love, be a true testament,
For in the journey of love, we grow and thrive,
And find joy in the balance that keeps our love alive.

Maintaining a healthy balance between autonomy and interdependence is key to a successful long-term love relationship. Autonomy refers to the ability to make decisions and take actions independently, while interdependence is the ability to rely on and support each other in a relationship.

Tips to help you navigate this delicate balance:

1. **Respect each other's independence:** It's important to respect each other's individuality and allow each other the freedom to pursue personal interests and goals. This can strengthen the relationship by creating a sense of mutual respect and admiration for each other's unique qualities and strengths.

2. **Maintain open communication:** Effective communication is essential for navigating the balance between autonomy and interdependence. Talk openly and honestly about your needs, wants, and boundaries. Listen actively and strive to understand each other's perspective.

3. **Find common ground:** While maintaining independence is important, finding common ground and shared interests can help build a strong foundation for the relationship. Explore new activities and experiences together and create shared goals that you can work towards.

4. **Practice compromise:** In any relationship, compromise is necessary. When conflicts arise, take the time to listen to each

other and work together to find a mutually beneficial solution. Be willing to make small sacrifices for the sake of the relationship.

5. **Respect each other's differences:** Everyone has their own unique personality, values, and beliefs. It's important to respect and embrace these differences in order to maintain a healthy balance of autonomy and interdependence.

By practicing these tips, you can create a healthy balance of autonomy and interdependence in your long-term love relationship, leading to a fulfilling and satisfying partnership.

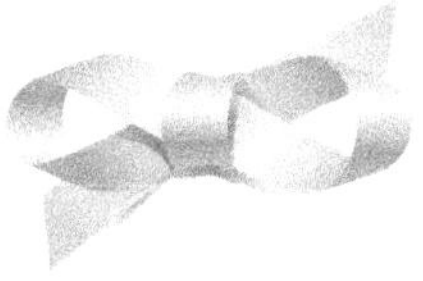

Chapter 13: Weathering Life's Challenges

Life's challenges can put a strain on even the strongest relationships, and long-term love is no exception. Whether it's the loss of a job, the death of a loved one, or a major health issue, couples need to be able to weather life's challenges together in order to maintain a strong emotional connection.

Life is full of challenges, and even the strongest relationships are not immune to them. However, couples who have developed a strong foundation of love and trust can often weather life's challenges with grace and resilience.

In the journey of love, where hearts are bound,
Life's challenges may come, and try to surround,
But when we weather them with strength,
Love grows deeper, and lasts at length.
Through the storms and trials of life's way,
Challenges may come, and try to sway,

But when we approach them hand in hand,
Our love endures, and forever stands.
For when we face challenges with love,
Our bond strengthens, like a velvet glove,
We learn to support and to console,
And build a love that will never grow old.
So let us weather life's challenges with care,
And let our love, forever flourish and share,
For in the journey of love, we grow and thrive,
And find joy in the challenges that keep our love alive.

Ways to help you and your partner navigate difficult times together

1. **Prioritize communication:** It is essential to communicate effectively during challenging times. Set aside time to discuss your concerns and fears openly and honestly. Be sure to listen to your partner's perspective with empathy and understanding.

2. **Support each other:** When one partner is struggling, the other should offer emotional support and encouragement. Make time to check in on each other regularly and offer help where needed.

3. **Practice self-care:** When faced with challenges, it can be easy to neglect self-care. However, taking care of your-self is essential for maintaining a healthy relationship. Make time for exercise, healthy eating, and relaxation to reduce stress.

4. **Seek outside support:** Sometimes, the support of family, friends, or a therapist can be beneficial. Consider reaching out to trusted loved ones or seeking professional help to work through challenging times together.

5. **Remember your shared goals:** During challenging times, it is easy to lose sight of your shared goals as a couple. Take time to remind each other of your long-term aspirations and how you can support each other in achieving them.

6. **Stay positive:** It can be difficult to maintain a positive outlook during challenging times, but staying positive can help you and your partner navigates difficulties together. Celebrate small victories and express gratitude for each other and the positive aspects of your life.

By prioritizing communication, offering support, practicing self-care, seeking outside help, remembering shared goals, and staying positive, you and your partner can weather life's challenges together and emerge stronger and more connected than ever.

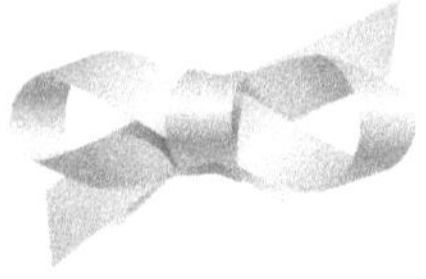

Chapter 14: Rediscovering Love

As couples navigate the ups and downs of long-term love, it's not uncommon for the initial spark and excitement of the relationship to fade over time. However, it's possible to rediscover and reignite that spark, by actively cultivating a sense of adventure, exploration, and connection in the relationship.

As time passes, it's natural for the initial passion and excitement of a relationship to wane. However, this doesn't mean that love has to fade away completely. In fact, many couples report feeling a deeper sense of love and connection as their relationship matures.

In the journey of love, where hearts entwine,
Long-term relationships can sometimes decline,
But when we rediscover love with zeal,
Our hearts ignite, and our love can heal.
Through the twists and turns of life's way,

Our love may falter, and sometimes sway,
But when we approach it with an open heart,
Our love revives, and never falls apart.
For when we rediscover love with grace,
Our bond deepens, and we find our place,
We learn to appreciate, and to see,
And build a love that's meant to be.
So let us rediscover love with care,
And let our hearts, forever cherish and share,
For in the journey of love, we grow and thrive,
And find joy in rediscovering, that keeps our love alive.

It you're in a long-term relationship and are looking to reignite the spark, there are several things you can do to rediscover love.

1. **Remember why you fell in love in the first place** -Take some time to reflect on the early days of your relationship. Think about what drew you to your partner and what qualities you admired. Recalling these memories can help you feel more positive and affectionate towards your partner.

2. **Spend quality time together** -In the busyness of daily life, it's easy to get caught up in work, chores, and other responsibilities. Make a conscious effort to carve out time for just the two of you. Plan date nights, take a weekend getaway, or simply have a movie night at home.

3. **Try new things together** -Trying something new can be exciting and can create shared experiences that can bring you closer together. Take a dance class, try a new hobby, or plan an adventure together.

4. **Express your love** -Sometimes it's easy to assume that your partner knows how you feel about them, but it's important to express your love and appreciation regularly. This can be done through words, actions, or small gestures of affection.

5. **Focus on the positive** -It's easy to get caught up in negativity

and focus on the things that bother you about your partner. Instead, try to focus on the positive aspects of your relationship and your partner's qualities that you admire.

6. **Practice forgiveness** -Holding onto grudges or resentment can create distance between you and your partner. Practice forgiveness and work towards resolving conflicts in a constructive and respectful way.

7. **Seek support** -If you're struggling to rediscover love in your relationship, consider seeking the support of a therapist or counselor. A professional can provide objective feedback and guidance to help you navigate the challenges of a long-term relationship.

Rediscovering love in a long-term relationship takes effort, but it's well worth it. By focusing on the positive, spending quality time together, and expressing your love and appreciation, you can reignite the spark and deepen your connection with your partner.

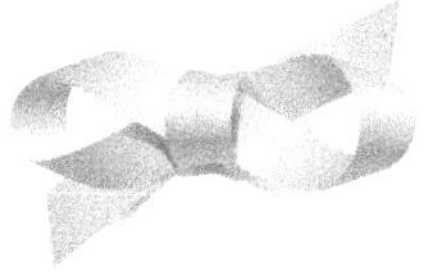

Chapter 15: Navigating Change and Growth

Long-term love relationships are inevitably affected by change and growth. As individuals, we are constantly changing and evolving, which can lead to changes in our relationships as well. Navigating these changes and growth can be a challenge, but it is crucial for the success and longevity of the relationship.

In the journey of love, where hearts entwine,
Change and growth can happen over time,
But when we navigate them with love,
Our bond deepens, and we rise above.
Through the ups and downs of life's way,
Change and growth may come, and try to sway,
But when we approach them hand in hand,
Our love endures, and forever stands.

For when we navigate change and growth with care,
Our love thrives, and we become a pair,
We learn to adapt and to evolve,
And build a love that will never dissolve.
So let us navigate change and growth with grace,
And let our love, forever have a place,
For in the journey of love, we grow and thrive,
And find joy in navigating change and growth that keeps our love alive.

Tips for navigating change and growth

1. **Embrace change:** Change is inevitable, and it can be scary. However, it's important to embrace it and view it as an opportunity for growth and development, both individually and as a couple. Change can bring new experiences, perspectives, and insights that can strengthen the relationship.

2. **Communicate openly:** Communication is key in any relationship, but especially when navigating change and growth. It's important to openly communicate your feelings, fears, and concerns with your partner. This can help to build trust and deepen your connection.

3. **Be flexible:** Being open and flexible to change is important in any relationship. It's important to be willing to adapt and compromise when needed to meet the changing needs of your partner and the relationship.

4. **Prioritize time together:** As life changes and evolves, it's easy to let time with your partner slip away. It's important to prioritize time together and make it a priority in your busy schedules. This can help to maintain the intimacy and connection in the relationship.

5. **Practice self-care:** Taking care of your-self is crucial in any relationship, but especially when navigating change and growth. Take time for yourself to recharge and focus on your own personal growth and development. This can help you to

be a better partner and navigate changes in the relationship with more ease.

By embracing change, communicating openly, being flexible, prioritizing time together, and practicing self-care, couples can successfully navigate the changes and growth that come with long-term love relationships.

Conclusion

In conclusion, maintaining a long-term love relationship requires effort, commitment, and a willingness to grow and change together over time. By prioritizing essential factors like effective communication, physical and emotional intimacy, mutual support and respect, and shared experiences and goals, couples can build a relationship that grows stronger and more fulfilling with each passing year.

However, it's also important to recognize that every relationship is unique, and there is no one "right" way to maintain a long-term love relationship. What works for one couple may not work for another and it's important to be flexible and adaptable in your approach.

Ultimately, the key to maintaining a strong and fulfilling long-term love relationship is to prioritize your connection with your partner, and to approach your relationship with a sense of openness, curiosity, and willingness to learn and grow together.

By doing so, you can build a relationship that brings you joy, fulfillment, and meaning for years to come.

In the relationship that brings me joy,

My heart sings, like a bird in joy,

For in your arms, I find my place,

And in your eyes, I see my grace.

Your love is like a raging fire,

That consumes me with intense desire,

And in your touch, I find release,

My soul ignites, like a masterpiece.

In your embrace, I feel complete,

Like two hearts, that forever meets,
Our love is like a symphony,
That echoes throughout eternity.
For in the relationship that brings me joy,
My heart dances, like a child's toy,
And in your love, I find my home,
Where I can forever roam.
So let us revel in this love divine,
And let our hearts, forever intertwine,
For in the relationship that brings us joy,
Our love endures, like a precious alloy.

Don't miss out!

Visit the website below and you can sign up to receive emails whenever Rajesh Giri publishes a new book. There's no charge and no obligation.

https://books2read.com/r/B-A-OWRS-UUZFC

BOOKS2READ

Connecting independent readers to independent writers.

Did you love *Still In Love With Her: A Guide To Sustain in a Long-Term Relationship*? Then you should read *Beyond Time and Space: A Love That Endures*[1] by Rajesh Giri!

"Beyond Time and Space: A Love That Endures" is a heartwarming and emotionally captivating love story that spans across time and space.

This book tells the story of two people who are separated by time and distance, yet are brought together by an unbreakable bond that defies all odds.The book takes readers on a journey through different eras and locations, from medieval times to modern-day New York City, and explores the challenges that come with a love that transcends time and space.With vivid descriptions and engaging characters, this book is a true page-turner that will leave readers rooting for the protagonists and

---

1. https://books2read.com/u/4ENay0

2. https://books2read.com/u/4ENay0

their enduring love.This book also delves into the deeper themes of love, fate, and destiny, making it a perfect read for those who enjoy thought-provoking stories.Whether you're a fan of romance novels or simply love a good story that touches the heart, "Beyond Time and Space: A Love That Endures" is a must-read.

Beyond Time and Space: A Love That Endures is a comprehensive guidebook that delves into the secrets of sustaining a loving and lasting relationship. This book contains factual chapters, examples of real-life love stories, and relaxing romantic poetry to help readers understand the importance of love and connection in their lives.

Through engaging activities, the book guides readers on how to maintain love and connection with their partners, no matter the challenges they may face. From the importance of communication and trust to the role of empathy and compassion, this book covers all the essential facts needed to sustain a healthy and fulfilling relationship.

Furthermore, the book features example love letters that teach readers how to communicate effectively and build a strong foundation for their relationships. These letters demonstrate the power of words and how they can bring people together in a profound and meaningful way.

Whether you're in a long-term relationship or just starting out, Beyond Time and Space: A Love That Endures is a must-read book. It provides practical advice, insightful wisdom, and heartfelt inspiration that will help you nurture your relationship and keep the flame of love burning brightly. So, if you're ready to discover the secrets of a happy and enduring love story, this book is the perfect place to start.

Check the thrilling love letter before reading the whole book

My dearest Reshma,

As I sit down to write this letter, I am filled with longing for your presence. Even though miles separate us, our love is stronger than the distance that separates us.

"My love for you is as boundless as the ocean,

As timeless as the tides,

And as deep as the sea."

Every day, my heart aches to be near you, to feel your touch and to hear your voice. But until then, I will let my words carry my love across time and space to you.

I remember the day we met like it was yesterday. The way you smiled at me, the sound of your laughter, and the sparkle in your eyes - I knew I had found my soulmate. And now, as I look back on our journey together, I realize that our love has grown even stronger with each passing day.

"We may be separated by distance and time,

But our love knows no bounds,

And our hearts beat as one."

Through the trials and tribulations of life, our love has remained steadfast and true. I know that no matter where we are or what challenges we may face, our love will endure.

So, my beloved Reshma, I make this promise to you - to love you, to cherish you, and to hold you close, even across time and space.

Forever yours,

Badal

Also by Rajesh Giri

Scamming in the Shoe Market: An Inside Look
Still In Love With Her: A Guide To Sustain in a Long-Term
Relationship
Beyond Time and Space: A Love That Endures

About the Author

Rajesh Kumar Giri is a renowned lecturer of Mathematics, content writer, and a Practical Success Coach. With a passion for writing academic and educational content, Rajesh guides and trains people worldwide, breaking the barriers of language and region with his simple and easy-to-understand writing skills.

Rajesh's journey began in a poor family in a remote area of West Champaran, where he faced numerous challenges in paying for higher education. Despite the obstacles, he persevered and completed his degree, taking his first steps towards educating people and sharing his rags-to-riches ideas. Today, he resides in New Delhi, the capital of India, with his beautiful wife and two lovely sons, and he remains dedicated to serving poor students by providing free education online and offline.

Rajesh has been writing content in the education, affiliate marketing, and health niches since 2006. He believes that experiences speak louder than imaginary and bookish ideas, and his words connect with readers and result in conversions. As a Practical Success Coach, he helps people overcome their limiting beliefs and achieve their goals through practical techniques and strategies.

With his wealth of experience and passion for writing, Rajesh is committed to helping people around the world unlock their full potential and achieve success in all areas of their lives.